Piano Lessons

BOOK 3

Revised Edition

FOREWORD

When music excites our interest and imagination, we eagerly put our hearts into learning it. The music in the **Hal Leonard Student Piano Library** encourages practice, progress, confidence, and best of all – success! Over 1,000 students and teachers in a nationwide test market responded with enthusiasm to the:

- variety of styles and moods
- natural rhythmic flow, singable melodies and lyrics
- "best ever" teacher accompaniments
- improvisations integrated throughout the **Lesson Books**
- instrumental accompaniments included in audio and MIDI formats.

When new concepts have an immediate application to the music, the effort it takes to learn these skills seems worth it. Test market teachers and students were especially excited about the:

- "realistic" pacing that challenges without overwhelming
- clear and concise presentation of concepts that allows room for a teacher's individual approach
- uncluttered page layout that keeps the focus on the music.

The **Piano Practice Games** books are preparation activities to coordinate technique, concepts, and creativity with the actual music in **Piano Lessons**. In addition, the **Piano Theory Workbook** presents fun writing activities for review, and the **Piano Solos** series reinforces concepts with challenging performance repertoire.

The **Hal Leonard Student Piano Library** is the result of the efforts of many individuals. We extend our gratitude to all the teachers, students and colleagues who shared their energy and creative input. May this method guide your learning as you bring this music to life.

Best wishes,

Barbara Kreader   Fred Kern   Phillip Keveren   Mona Rejino

Authors
Barbara Kreader, Fred Kern, Phillip Keveren, Mona Rejino

Consultants
Tony Caramia, Bruce Berr, Richard Rejino

Illustrator
Fred Bell

To access audio, visit:
www.halleonard.com/mylibrary

Enter Code
4900-3895-4736-3443

ISBN 978-0-634-03120-5

HAL•LEONARD®

Visit Hal Leonard Online at
www.halleonard.com

World headquarters, contact:
Hal Leonard
7777 West Bluemound Road
Milwaukee, WI 53213
Email: info@halleonard.com

In Europe, contact:
Hal Leonard Europe Limited
1 Red Place
London, W1K 6PL
Email: info@halleonardeurope.com

In Australia, contact:
Hal Leonard Australia Pty. Ltd.
4 Lentara Court
Cheltenham, Victoria, 3192 Australia
Email: info@halleonard.com.au

REVIEW OF BOOK TWO

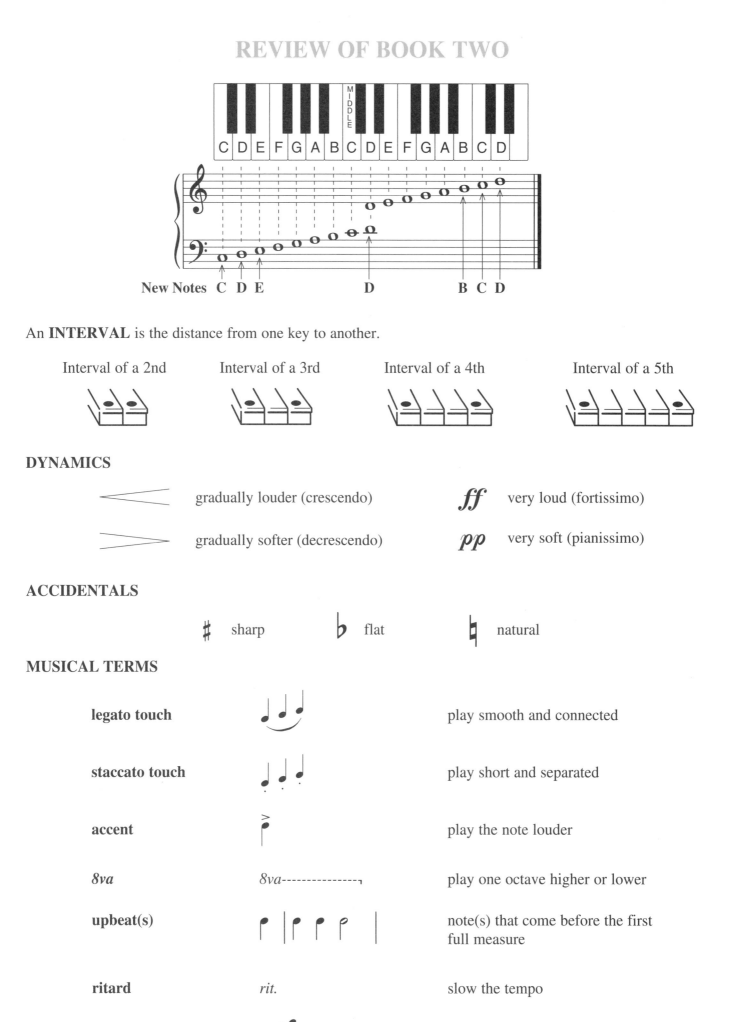

An **INTERVAL** is the distance from one key to another.

Interval of a 2nd	Interval of a 3rd	Interval of a 4th	Interval of a 5th

DYNAMICS

         gradually louder (crescendo)   *ff*   very loud (fortissimo)

         gradually softer (decrescendo)   *pp*   very soft (pianissimo)

ACCIDENTALS

     ♯   sharp   ♭   flat   ♮   natural

MUSICAL TERMS

legato touch		play smooth and connected
staccato touch		play short and separated
accent		play the note louder
8va	*8va---------------*	play one octave higher or lower
upbeat(s)		note(s) that come before the first full measure
ritard	*rit.*	slow the tempo
ledger lines		are added to notes written above or below the staff

CONTENTS

* Students can check pieces as they play them.

EIGHTH NOTES

Two **Eighth Notes** fill the time of one quarter note.

♩ = 1 beat

♫ = 1 beat

Clap and count these patterns:

1 & 2 & 3 & 4 &

Little River Flowing

Folk Tune

Smoothly

It is helpful to clap the rhythm of a piece before playing it.

mf Lit-tle riv-er flow-ing, flow-ing, flow-ing. Lit-tle riv-er flow-ing, flow-ing to the sea.

Lit-tle riv-er flow-ing, flow-ing to the sea.

Accompaniment (Student plays one octave higher than written.) 🔊 1/2

Smoothly (♩ = 100)

4

Dakota Melody

With a steady beat

Second time both hands play one octave lower.

American

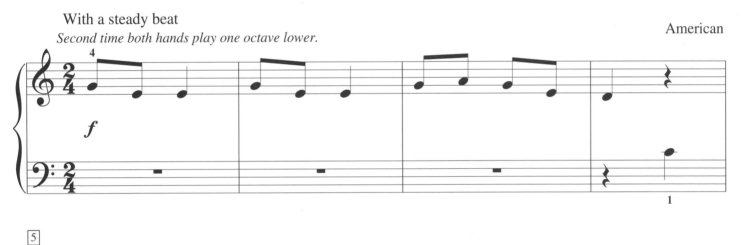

Accompaniment

With a steady beat (♩ = 86) 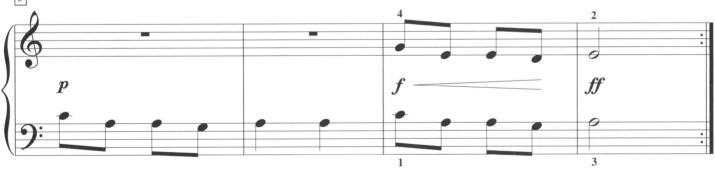 **3/4**

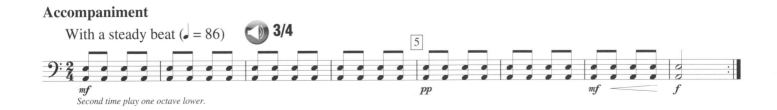

Second time play one octave lower.

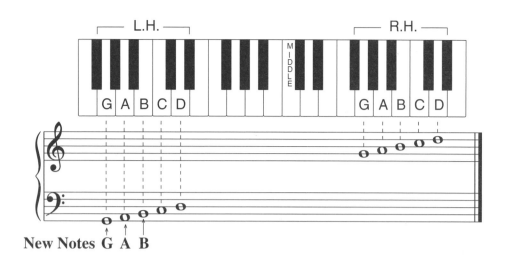

New Notes G A B

Follow The Leader

Phillip Keveren

Little Bird

Allegro (♩ = 145) **7/8**

German

mf Lit - tle bird, come and tell me what your song tries to say. Are you

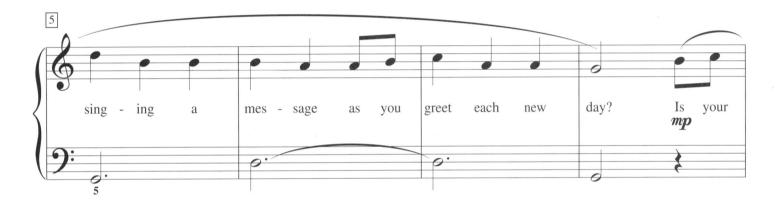

sing - ing a mes - sage as you greet each new day? Is your
mp

song al - ways hap - py? Do you some - times feel mad? Does your
f   mf

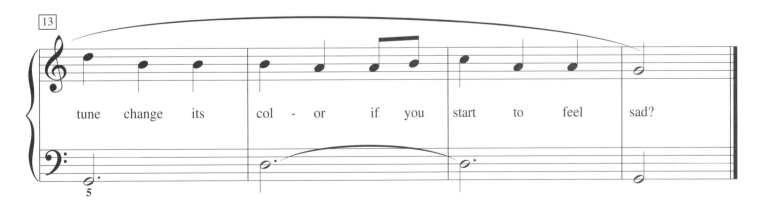

tune change its col - or if you start to feel sad?

Lullaby

Andante (♩ = 98)  9/10

Polish Folk Tune

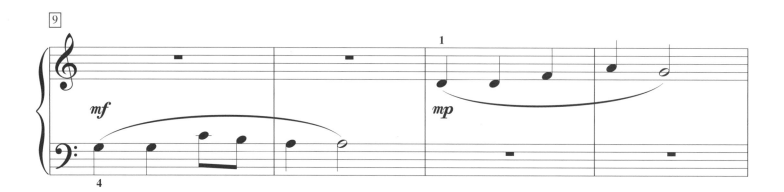

INTERVAL of a 6th

On the piano, a 6th
- skips four keys
- skips four letters

On the staff, a 6th
- skips four notes from either a line to a space or a space to a line.

Shortbread Boogie

Traditional
Arranged by Mona Rejino

Accompaniment (Student plays one octave higher than written.) 🔊 **11/12**

Lavender Mood

Folk Melody
Arranged by Phillip Keveren

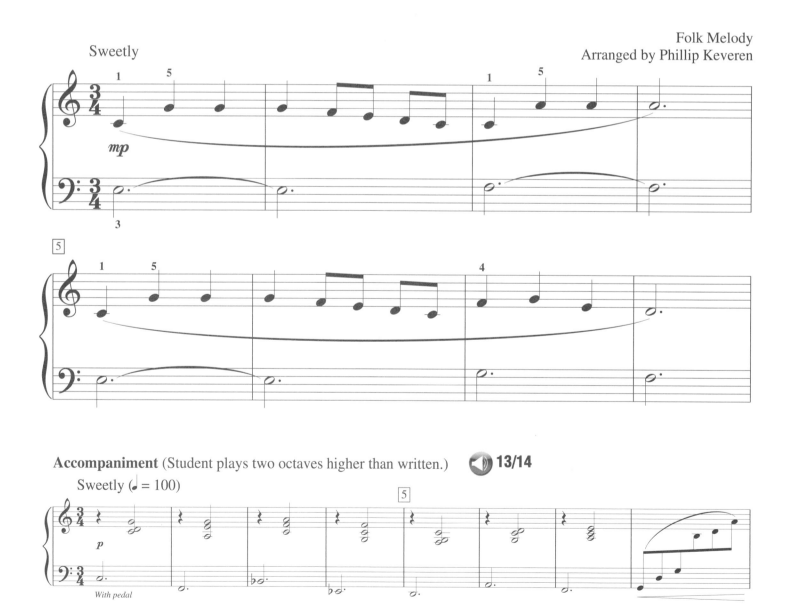

Accompaniment (Student plays two octaves higher than written.) 13/14

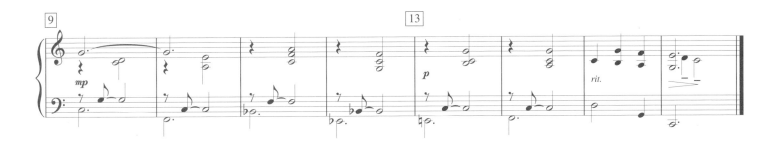

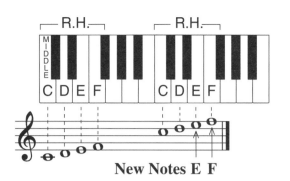

New Notes E F

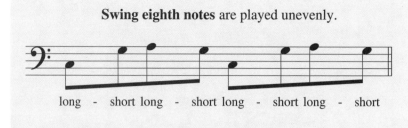

Swing eighth notes are played unevenly.

long - short long - short long - short long - short

Casey Jones

Music by Eddie Newton
Words by T. Lawrence Seibert
Arranged by Phillip Keveren

With a swing (♩ = 110)   15/16

*Start slowly as you leave the station
and build up speed gradually.*

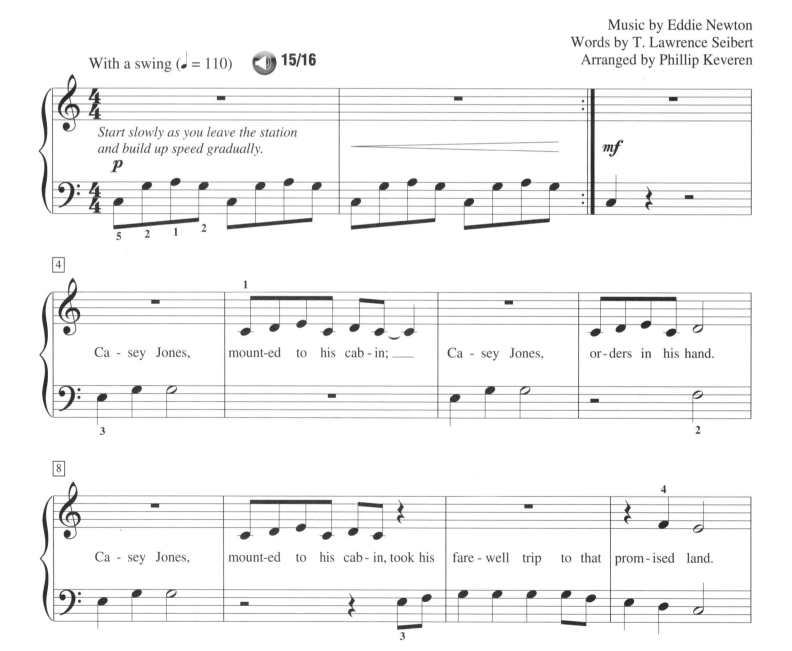

Ca - sey Jones, mount-ed to his cab-in; _____ Ca - sey Jones, or-ders in his hand.

Ca - sey Jones, mount-ed to his cab-in, took his fare - well trip to that prom-ised land.

Ca - sey Jones, mount-ed to his cab - in; ___ Ca - sey Jones, or - ders in his hand.

Ca - sey Jones, mount-ed to his cab - in, took his fare - well trip to that prom - ised land.

Gradually slow down.

Train whistle

Hold pedal down - - - -

13

Take Me Out To The Ball Game

Words by Jack Norworth
Music by Albert von Tilzer
Arranged by Fred Kern

With energy

f Take me out to the ball game.

Take me out with the crowd. _____

Buy me some pea - nuts and Crack - er Jack.

I don't care if I nev - er get back. Let me

Accompaniment (Student plays one octave higher than written.) 🔊 **17/18**

With energy (♩ = 150)

mf

14

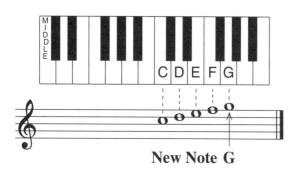
New Note G

Spring

Antonio Vivaldi
(1678–1741)
Adapted by Fred Kern

Allegro (♩ = 155) 19/20

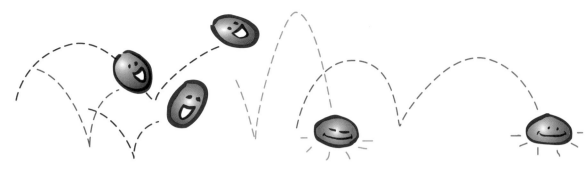

Bounces

Allegro (♩ = 200) 🔊 **21/22**   Italo Taranta

**DOTTED-QUARTER
EIGHTH NOTE**

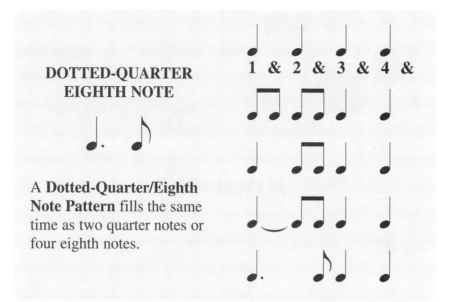

A **Dotted-Quarter/Eighth
Note Pattern** fills the same
time as two quarter notes or
four eighth notes.

Alouette

French
Arranged by Phillip Keveren

Accompaniment (Student plays one octave higher than written.) 23/24

Playfully ($\downarrow$ = 120)

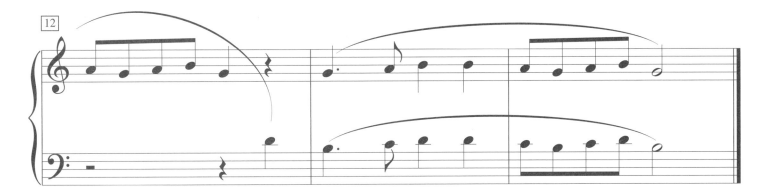

The Last Word

Quarrelsome (♩ = 145) **25/26**

Phillip Keveren

*(R.H. or L.H.)

Play a cluster of notes up high on the piano with the hand you think should have the last word!

HALF STEPS

A **Half Step** is the distance from one key to the next key, either higher or lower, black or white, **with no key between.**

Examples of half steps are:

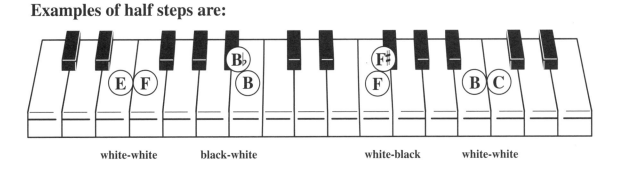

white-white   black-white   white-black   white-white

Monkey Business

Quickly

Notice that the first line of this song uses only half steps.

Traditional

$\boldsymbol{f}$ *On repeat, play gradually faster.*

Accompaniment (Student plays one octave higher than written.)   27/28

Quickly ($\quarternote$ = 170)

mf

21

Dixieland Jam

Quickly (♩ = 190) 🔊 **29/30**

Bill Boyd

Second time R.H. 8va

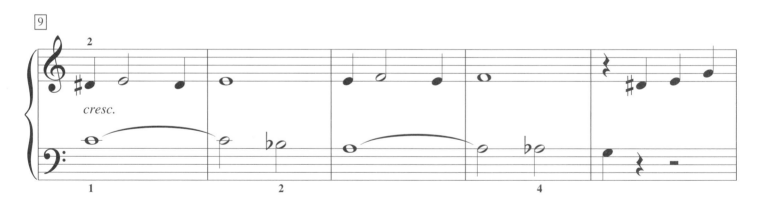

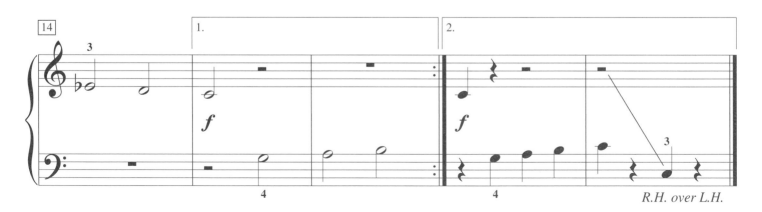

R.H. over L.H.

WHOLE STEPS

A **Whole Step** is the distance from one key to another, either higher or lower, black or white, with one key between.

One whole step = two half steps

Examples of whole steps are:

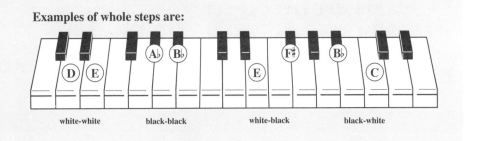

white-white   black-black   white-black   black-white

Setting Sun

Moderately slow, expressively (♩ = 125) **31/32**

Phillip Keveren

*pedal down   hold pedal down   pedal up

**a tempo* means return to the original tempo

MAJOR FIVE-FINGER PATTERNS

All **Major Five-Finger Patterns** are made up of five tones in the following order of half steps and whole steps.

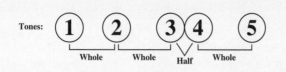

MAJOR TRIADS
(three-note chords)

Major Triads are made up of tones 1, 3 and 5 of any major five-finger pattern.

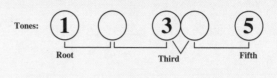

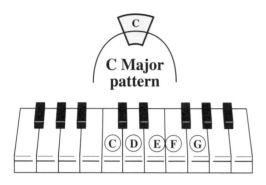

C Major triad

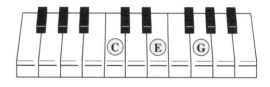

ARPEGGIOS

Arpeggios are notes of a broken chord played one after another, up or down a keyboard. One way to play arpeggios is hand-over-hand.

C Major Warm-Up

C Major Arpeggio

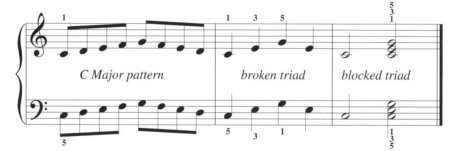

*(1st time *mf*, 2nd time *p*)

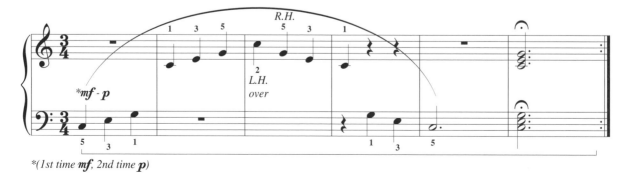

24

My Own Song
Improvisation (Improv) in C Major

Place both hands in the **C Major five-finger pattern**. As your teacher plays the accompaniment below, improvise a melody using one hand or the other.

Barefoot On
A Hot Sidewalk

Key of C Major
Key Signature: *no sharps or flats*

Allegro (♩ = 132)   34/35

Phillip Keveren

March

Antonio Diabelli
(1781–1858)
Arranged by Fred Kern

Allegro (♩ = 132) 36/37

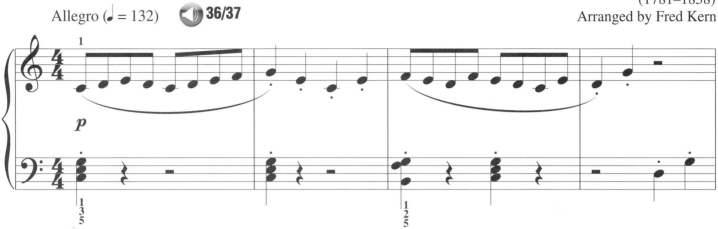

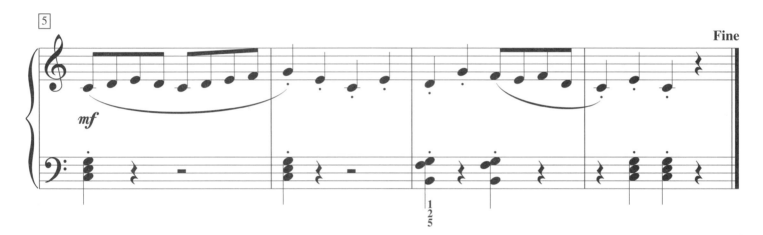

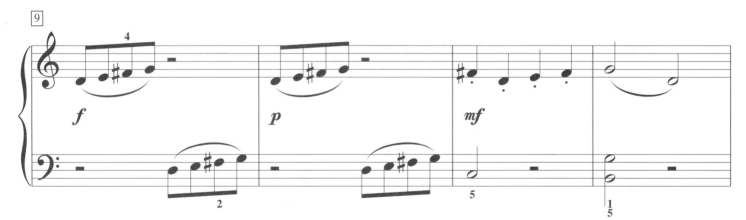

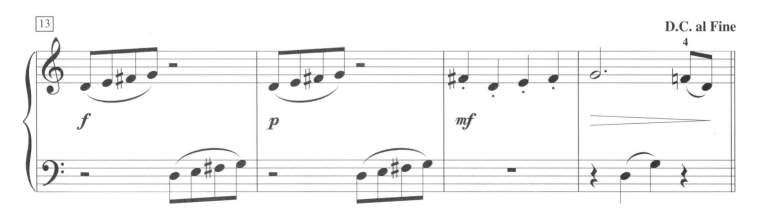

Handoff

Steady (swing eighths)

Mona Rejino

Accompaniment (Student plays one octave higher than written.)

Steady (swing eighths) (♩ = 116) 38/39

Every major five-finger pattern has a related minor five-finger pattern.
C Major and A minor are related.

MINOR FIVE-FINGER PATTERNS

All **Minor Five-Finger Patterns** are made up of five tones in the following order of half steps and whole steps.

MINOR TRIADS
(three-note chords)

Minor Triads are made up of tones 1, 3 and 5 of any minor five-finger pattern.

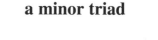

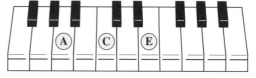

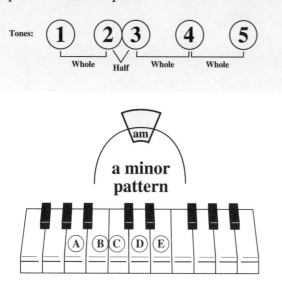

a minor triad

A Minor Warm-Up

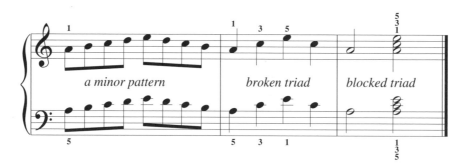

a minor pattern *broken triad* *blocked triad*

A Minor Arpeggio

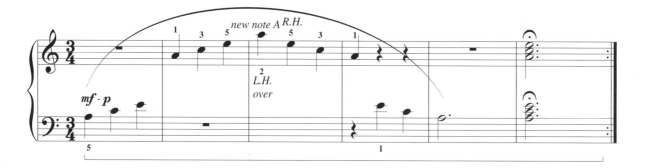

My Own Song
Improv in A Minor

As your teacher plays the accompaniment below, improvise a melody using the **a minor five-finger pattern**.

Street Fair

RELATED KEY SIGNATURES

Related major and minor five-finger patterns use the same key signature. The key signatures for C Major and a minor have no sharps or flats.

Key of A minor
Key signature: *no sharps or flats*

Armenian Folk Tune

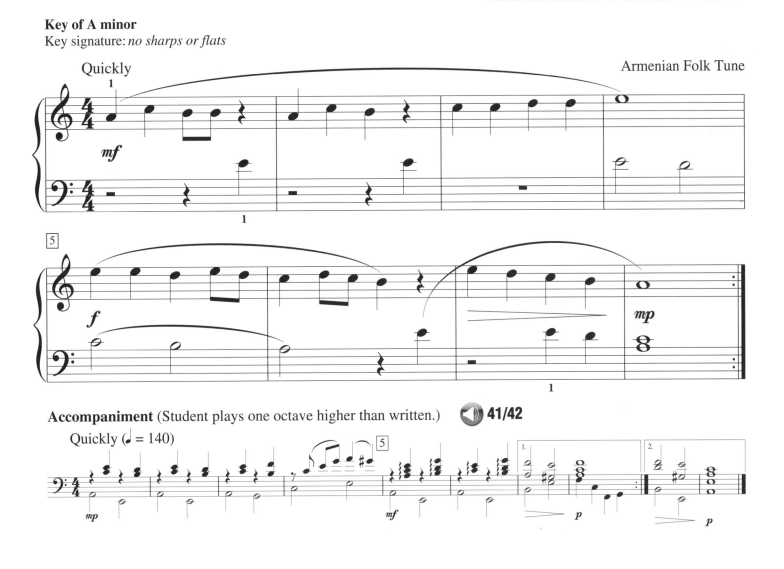

Accompaniment (Student plays one octave higher than written.) 41/42

Penguin Heat Wave

Allegro (♩ = 144) 43/44

Mona Rejino

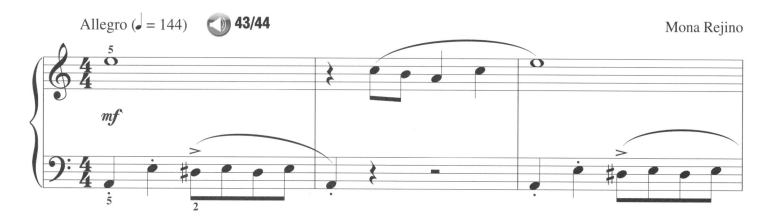

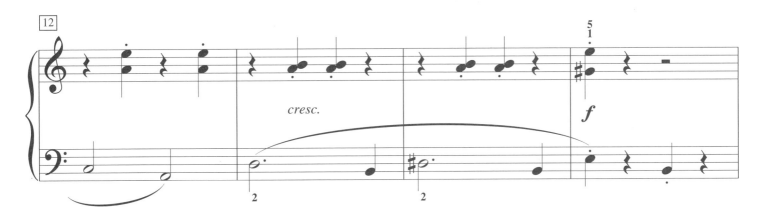

In Concert

Fred Kern and
Phillip Keveren

Grandiose (♩. = 63)   45/46

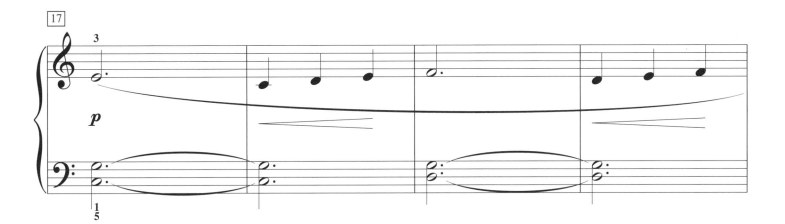

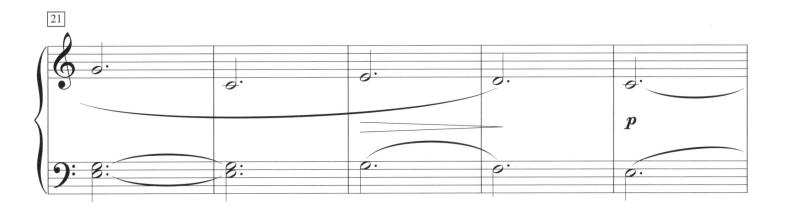

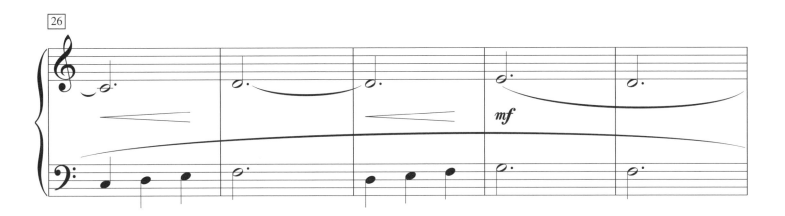

D.C. al Fine

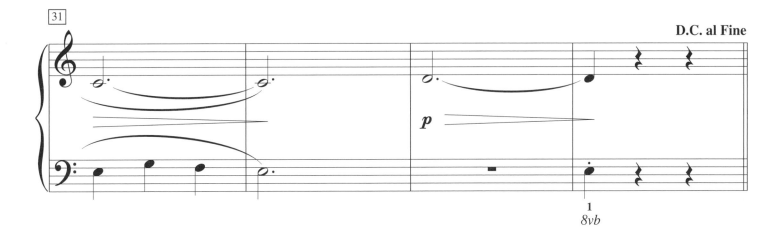

33

G Major Warm-Up

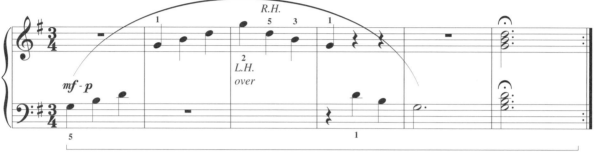

G Major pattern   *broken triad*   *blocked triad*

G Major Arpeggio

My Own Song
Improv in G Major

Place both hands in the **G Major five-finger pattern**. As your teacher plays the accompaniment below, improvise a melody using one hand or the other.

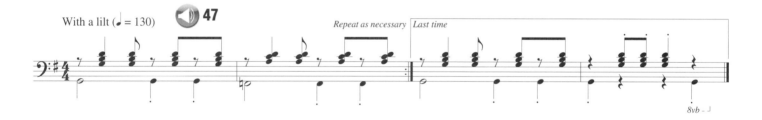

TRANSPOSITION

A piece can be played in any key. The notes will be different, but the intervals and the rhythms will be the same. This is called **Transposition**.

You already know how to play "Barefoot On A Hot Sidewalk" (page 25) in the C Major pattern. Now play the piece in the G Major pattern.

Barefoot On A Hot Sidewalk

etc.

34

Steps Before Sight Reading and Playing

1. Where do I put my hands on the keyboard?
2. How will I count?
3. What is the direction and distance of each interval?

SIGHT READING

Sight Reading is when you play and "perform" a piece of music without practicing it first.

• Play each of the following examples as accurately as possible the first time.

• Play to the end of each example without stopping, even if you have to make up some notes to keep the beat.

• Count two measures in a medium tempo before you begin.

a.

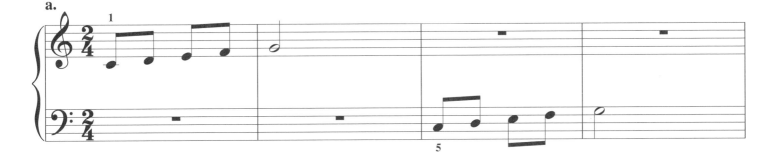

b.

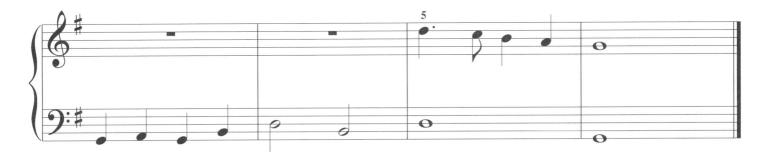

35

D.S. (Dal Segno) al Fine

means to return to 𝄋 (segno)
and play to the end (fine).

Moderato

Key of G Major

Key signature: *one sharp, F♯*

Heinrich Wohlfahrt
(1797–1883)
Op. 87 No. 47
Arranged by Fred Kern

Moderato

Accompaniment (Student plays one octave higher than written.)   48/49

Moderato (♩ = 140)

36

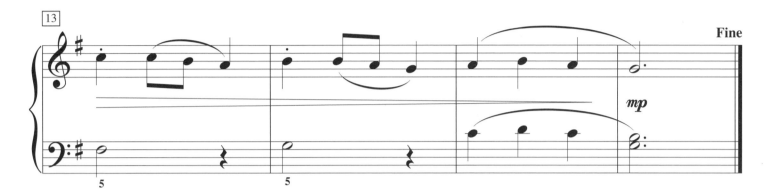

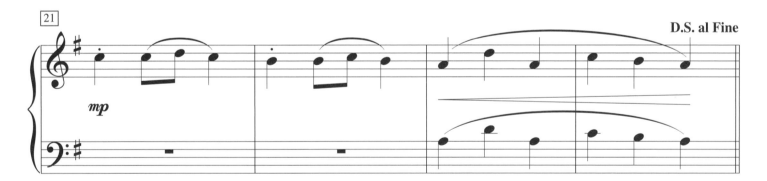

E Minor Warm-Up

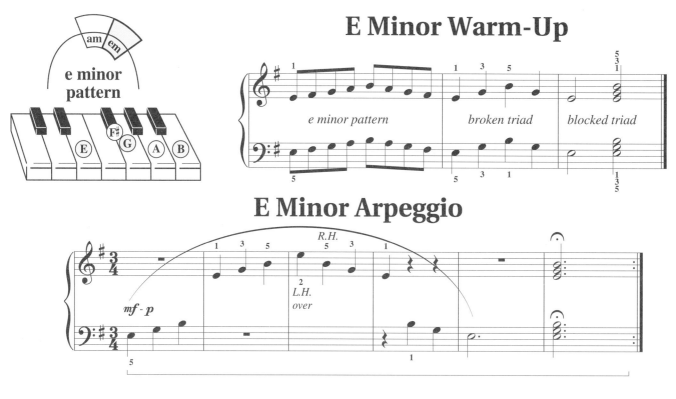

e minor pattern

e minor pattern   *broken triad*   *blocked triad*

E Minor Arpeggio

mf - p   R.H.   L.H. over

My Own Song

Improv in E Minor

As your teacher plays the accompaniment below, improvise a melody using the **e minor five-finger pattern**.

Allegro (♩ = 135) **50**

Repeat as necessary *Last time*

Searching

Andante (♩ = 60) **51/52**

Phillip Keveren

p   *mp*   *f*

6

p rit.   *pp*

New Note E →

Sight Reading

- Play each of the following examples as accurately as possible the first time.
- Play to the end of each example without stopping, even if you have to make up some notes to keep the beat.
- Count two measures in a medium tempo before you begin.

G Major

A minor

(Transpose to C Major)

(Transpose to E minor)

E minor

(Transpose to A minor)

Alla Turca

Antonio Diabelli
(1781–1858)
Op. 149 No. 26
Arranged by Fred Kern

Allegro (♩ = 140) 53/54

Zum Gali Gali

Israeli Folk Tune
Arranged by Fred Kern

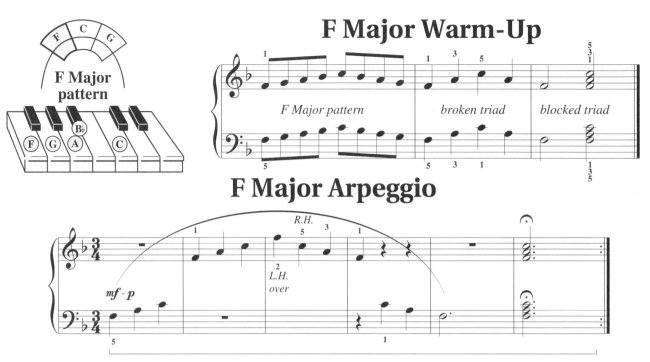

F Major Warm-Up

F Major Arpeggio

My Own Song
Improv in F Major

Place both hands in the F Major five-finger pattern. As your teacher plays the accompaniment below, improvise a melody using one hand or the other.

Playing Around a Sequence of Major Five-Finger Patterns

Beginning with F and moving clockwise around the circle, play:

F   C   G

Play the following patterns with your right hand.
Play all five notes of each pattern in one impulse, using a drop/lift motion of the wrist.
Let your arm follow your fingers.

Beginning on the F two octaves below Middle C, play the patterns again, using your left hand.

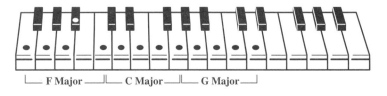

Beginning on any F on the keyboard, play the patterns hands together.

Alexander March

Key of F Major
Key signature: *one flat, B♭*
Brisk, walking tempo (♩ = 144) **58/59**

Ludwig van Beethoven
(1770–1827)
adapted by Barbara Kreader

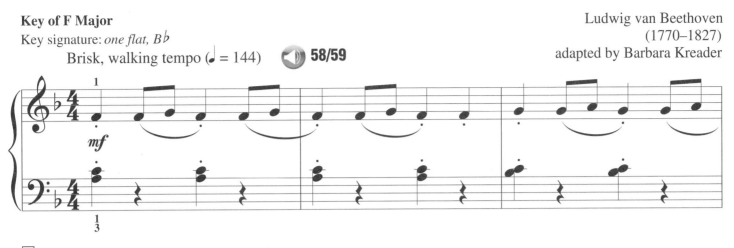

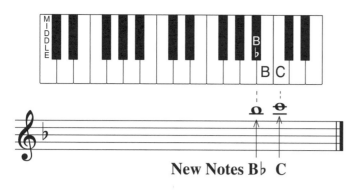

New Notes B♭ C

Chorale

Slowly (♩ = 88) 🔊 **60/61**

Fred Kern

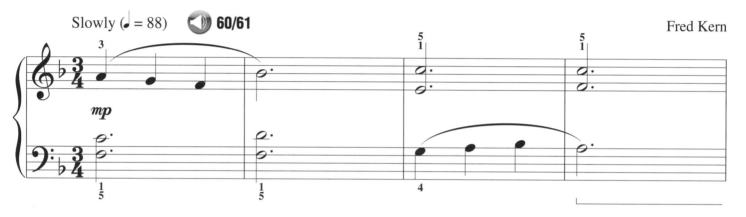

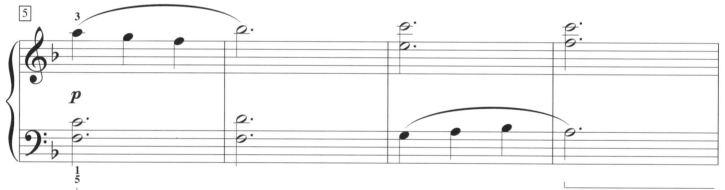

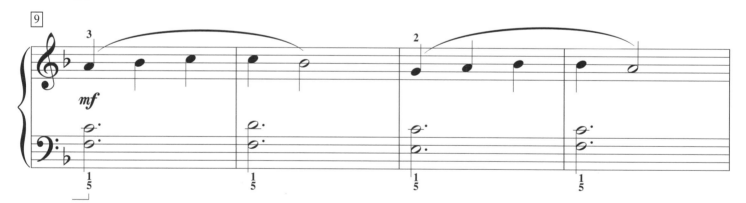

D Minor Warm-Up

D Minor Arpeggio

My Own Song
Improv in D Minor

As your teacher plays the accompaniment below, improvise a melody using the **d minor five-finger pattern**.

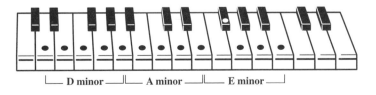

Playing Around a Sequence of Minor Five-Finger Patterns

Beginning with Dm and moving clockwise around the circle, play:

dm   **am**   **em**

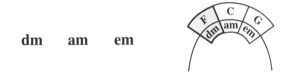

Play the following patterns with your right hand.
Play all five notes of each pattern in one impulse, using a drop/lift motion of the wrist.
Let your arm follow your fingers.

Beginning on the D two octaves below Middle C, play the patterns again, using your left hand.

Beginning on any D on the keyboard, play the patterns hands together.

45

In The Hall Of The Mountain King
from PEER GYNT

Key of D minor
Key signature: *one flat, B♭*

Edvard Grieg
(1843–1907)
Arranged by Phillip Keveren

March

Accompaniment (Student plays one octave higher than written.)

March (♩ = 104)

46

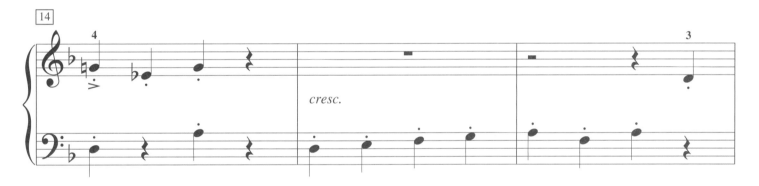

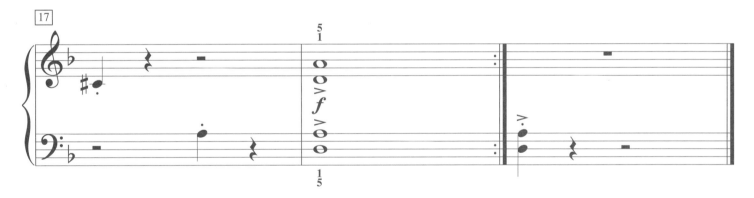

Floating

65/66

Fred Kern and
Brenda Dillon

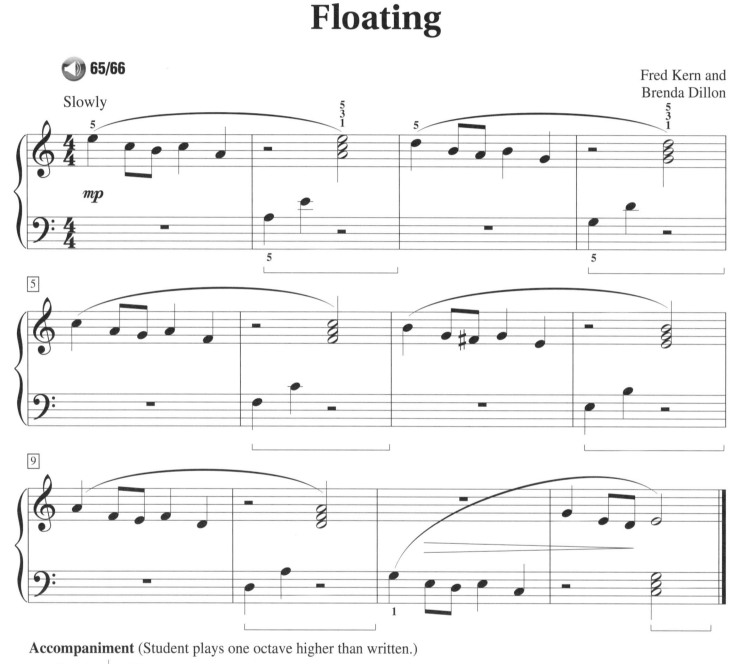

Accompaniment (Student plays one octave higher than written.)

The **Blues** is a type of American popular music that began in the first decade of the 20th century. An important feature of the blues style is a 12-bar harmonic pattern:

C/C/C/C   F/F/C/C   G/F/C/C

COMMON TIME

C

Common Time is another name for $\frac{4}{4}$.

You Can't Lose With The Blues

Swing it! (Swing eighths) ($\quarternote$ = 104)   67/68

Phillip Keveren

Every major five-finger pattern has
a parallel minor five-finger pattern.
They share the same keynote.

To change a major five-finger pattern to a minor
pattern, **lower the third tone** of the major pattern
one half step.

To change a minor five-finger pattern to a major
pattern, **raise the third tone** of the minor pattern
one half step.

Moody Hues

Steady (♩ = 100) 🔊 **69/70**

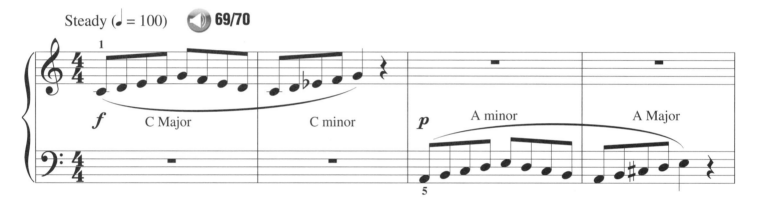

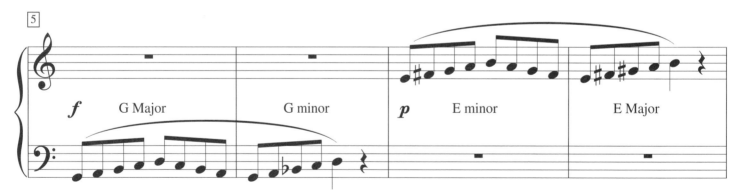

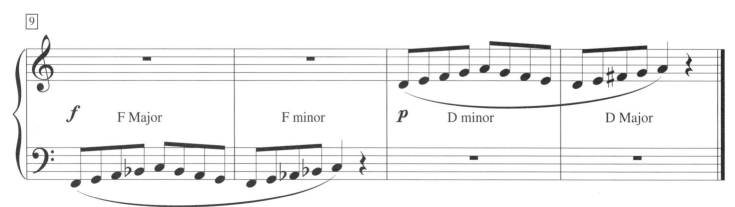

1. Play "Moody Hues" staccato.   2. Play two-note slurs.   3. Play hands together.

Joy

71/72

With energy (♩ = 155)

Barbara Kreader

Hold down damper pedal throughout.

Olé

With spirit (♩ = 176)   🔊 **73/74**

Mona Rejino

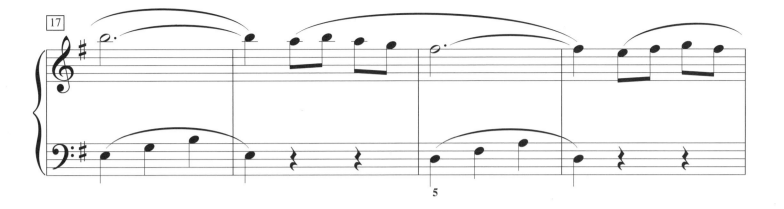

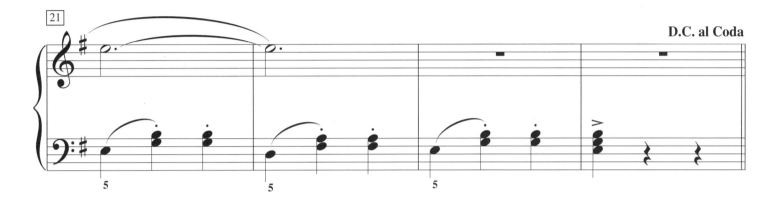

D.C. al Coda

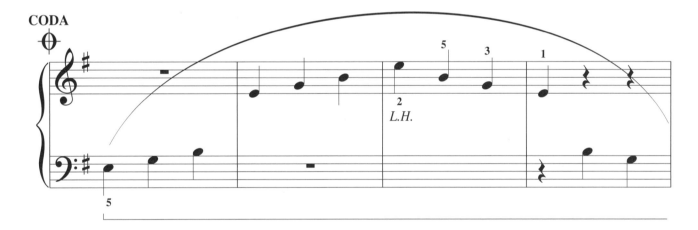

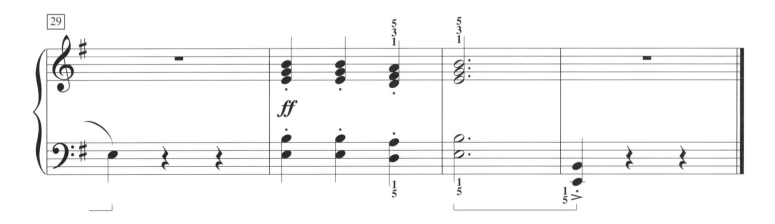

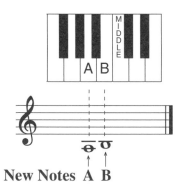

New Notes A B

15ma ⌐

When the sign *15ma-*⌐ appears over a note or group of notes, play the note or notes two octaves higher than written.

Fresh Start

With energy (♩ = 165) 🔊 **75/76**

Fred Kern

sempre staccato

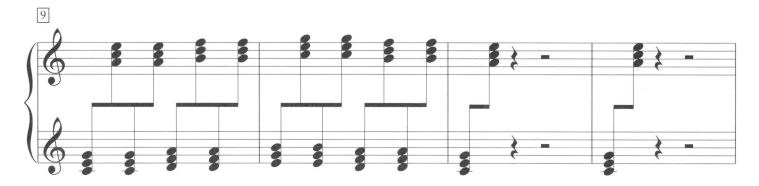

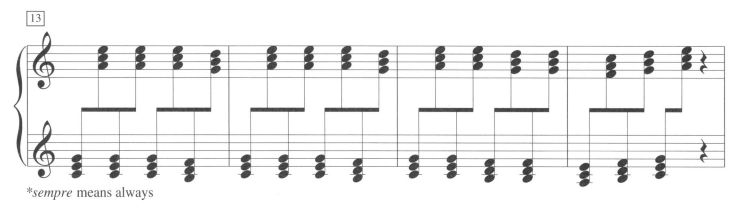

*sempre means always

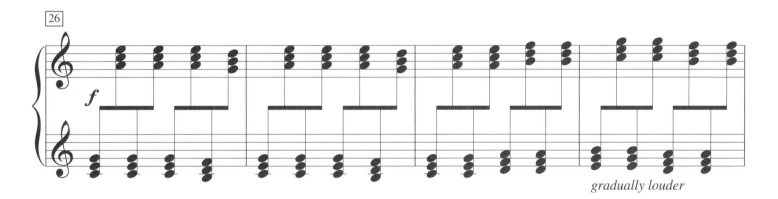

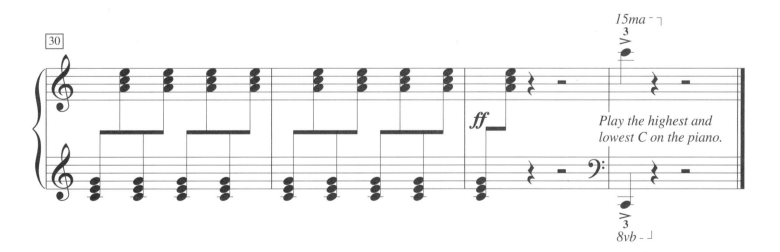

Play the highest and lowest C on the piano.

HAS SUCCESSFULLY COMPLETED
HAL LEONARD PIANO LESSONS,
BOOK THREE
AND
IS HEREBY PROMOTED TO
BOOK FOUR.

TEACHER   DATE

HAL•LEONARD®